THE MOUNTAIN GORILLA

Melissa Kim

Illustrated by
Ann Strugnell

Riverswift

London

First published by Hutchinson Children's Books in 1994

1 3 5 7 9 10 8 6 4 2

Melissa Kim and Ann Strugnell have asserted their right under the Copyright, Designs and Patents Act, 1988, to be identified as the author and illustrator of this work

This edition first published in 1995 by Riverswift
Random House, 20 Vauxhall Bridge Road, London SW1V 2SA

Random House Australia (Pty) Limited
20 Alfred Street, Milsons Point, Sydney
New South Wales 2061, Australia

Random House New Zealand Limited
18 Poland Road, Glenfield
Auckland 10, New Zealand

Random House South Africa (Pty) Limited
PO Box 337, Bergvlei, South Africa

Random House UK Limited Reg. No. 954009

Conceived, edited, designed and produced by Signpost Books, Ltd
25 Eden Drive, Headington, Oxford OX3 0AB

Editor: Dorothy Wood
Designer: Gillian Riley

A CIP catalogue record for this book is available from the British Library

ISBN 1 898304 74 2

Printed in Hong Kong

NOTICE TO QUIT

Please move out of your home at once. We do not know where you will find a warm enough climate or the right sort of food for you to eat but we need your space, so you have to go.

The Management

Wouldn't it be terrible if this happened to you and your family? Yet every year, week, day, some kind of living creature is disappearing from the world, because it is forced to leave its natural home.

The mountain gorilla, for example, is in serious danger. It may seem far away and remote, but you can help prevent this magnificent animal from becoming extinct.

If you care about animals in danger, you automatically become a Wildlifer. Wildlifers are people who share a common concern for animals and want to do something to make the world a better place for the mountain gorilla and for all of us.

Great ape family

CHIMPANZEES

Gorillas are the largest members of the GREAT APE FAMILY, which includes chimpanzees and orang-utans. The great apes belong to the animal order known as **primates**, which includes monkeys and humans. The great apes are our closest animal relatives. Primates are mammals. Mammals are warm-blooded animals that produce milk to feed their babies. The babies of gorillas, chimpanzees, and orang-utans spend several years with their parents.

GORILLAS

FACT FILE
Gorillas have no natural enemies apart from Man.

ORANG UTANS

The gorilla file

Not all gorillas are alike. Gorillas fall into three main types, according to their size, habits, and where they live. Lowland gorillas live on plains and at the base of mountains. Mountain gorillas live high up in the mountains, sometimes as high as 3500 metres (11,500 feet).

A

B

C

FACT FILE

Who's who here? Look at the descriptions. Decide which gorilla is which. Then look for the answer on page 32.

Mountain gorillas have been endangered for many years. Finding out about them and why they are endangered is like putting together a puzzle. To find all the pieces we will need to ask a series of questions.

Name: Western Lowland Gorilla

Address:	**Important features:**
Africa	Short black hair
Lives mainly in Cameroon,	Wide skull
Central African Republic,	Long arms and legs
Gabon, and the Congo	Thin hands
	Wide hips

Population: Estimated at about 39,000

Name: Eastern Lowland Gorilla

Address:	**Important features:**
Africa	Fairly short dark hair
Lives mainly in Zaire,	Narrow skull
Uganda	Long arms
	Thin hands
	Wide hips

Population: ENDANGERED Estimated between 3000 and 5000

Name: Mountain Gorilla

Address:	**Important features:**
Africa	Long, thick black hair
Lives mainly in mountains	Broad, long jaw
of Virunga Volcanoes area	Short arms and legs
where Uganda, Rwanda	Long torso
and Zaire intersect.	Short, broad hands
Some also live in Bwindi	Thin hips
Forest in Uganda	

Population: ENDANGERED Estimated at about 600

Where can mountain gorillas be found?

A mountain gorilla is a rare sight. This elusive animal can only be found in one small corner of this world.

Look carefully at this map of Africa.

- Can you find Zaire, Uganda and Rwanda (pronounced ru-WAN-da)?

- Place a sheet of tracing paper over the map and colour in these three countries.

- Make a circle around the spot where the three countries meet. These are the Virunga Mountains where the mountain gorillas live.

How many are there?

Hundreds of years ago **mountain gorillas** roamed around parts of central Africa. But by the 1950s there were only about 500 of them left. In 1982, scientists counted about 255 in the Virunga Volcanoes area and 120 in the Bwindi forest. Since then, the mountain gorilla population has slowly risen, though there are still only about 600 left (about 300 in the Virungas in Rwanda and Zaire, and about 308 in Bwindi, in Uganda).

The number of **lowland gorillas** is harder to discover. Many lowland gorillas live in forests too isolated for humans to explore easily. However, scientists feel sure that there are more lowland than mountain gorillas.

Some gorillas live in zoos. Most of the gorillas in zoos are **western lowland gorillas**. Only about 10 to 15 **eastern lowland gorillas** live in zoos.

Counting gorillas in the wild is not easy. Scientists use several different methods to track, identify, and count different gorilla groups.

Some scientists have actually lived with gorillas. They get to know each gorilla individually. This is the best way to keep track of a population, but it's difficult to do this for every single group of gorillas, as some live in places where humans would find it difficult to survive.

FACT FILE

One way scientists estimate how many gorillas there are in an area is to count the signs they leave behind.

Solve this puzzle and find the exact number of mountain gorillas counted in a recent survey.

  Foot print

Thumb print

  Knuckle print

Count the prints:

Foot prints	_ _ _ _ × 100
Thumb prints	_ _ _ _ × 10
Knuckle prints	_ _ _ _ × 1

Total number of mountain gorillas.

(Answers on page 32.)

Let's see how many gorillas we can find in this picture.

Minimum number = The number of gorillas we can actually see.

Maximum number = The number of signs the gorillas have left behind plus the number of gorillas you can see.

Gorilla Signs

Nest

Droppings

Flattened Plants

Food remains   Knuckle prints

How many gorillas do you see?

How many signs can you find?

What are your maximum and minimum numbers?

(Answers on page 32.)

11

What are mountain gorillas like?

If you have a picture in your mind of gorillas as noisy, ferocious beasts, put it aside. They are actually very peaceable animals, and not at all dangerous. They rarely fight with each other, and they certainly don't fight anyone else.

FACT FILE

Beating the chest is part of a 'display'. There are nine parts to a display. Only the **silverbacks**, the male gorillas who act as leaders of a group, perform all nine parts. Others may perform only a few of the parts.

- Hoot
- Pretend to eat
- Rise on two legs
- Throw plants
- Beat chest
- Kick legs
- Run around
- Hit or tear out plants
- Thump on the ground

Usually, gorillas make a display when they're afraid, or when they think one of them is about to be hurt. It's mostly noise and arm-waving, and it's meant to scare off the person or animal that they're afraid of.

All mountain gorillas live in groups. These groups, which are like large families, are very important to the gorilla's way of life. It is difficult for a gorilla to live without a group for ever, though males may spend many years alone.

Gorilla groups often include females from several different families, so not all the members are actually related by blood. A group with about 30 members has been seen, but the average group has eight to ten members.

Each group has a leader. He protects the group. He decides when and where the group travels, rests, eats, and sleeps.

The leader is one of the older males, called a silverback. As male gorillas get older, the hair on their backs turns from black to grey, or silver. Usually, there's one silverback in each group.

The group also includes black-backed males, females with babies, single females, and young gorillas. The babies cling to their mothers' bellies, then, when they are a little older, they ride on their mothers' backs.

FAMILY ALBUM

This holds the personal information of a young adult mountain gorilla.

Name:	Kimbo
GROUP DATA	
Number in Group:	9
Group Leader's Name:	Silverback
Group Leader's Height:	1.75 metres
PERSONAL DATA	
Weight at birth:	2 kilos
Current weight:	120 kilos
Height:	1.4 metres
Age:	9 years

Make your own personal and family information sheet and fill it in.

FAMILY ALBUM

Name:
GROUP DATA

Number in Group:
Group Leader's Name:
Group Leader's Height:
PERSONAL DATA
Weight at birth:
Current weight:
Height:
Age:

Adult males, aged 10 to 14 years, weigh about 150 kilos (330 pounds), twice as much as an average female. The average male is about 1.7 metres tall (5ft 8in).

A day in the life of a gorilla

6.30–7.30 am: Wake up (half an hour after sunrise).

7.30–10.45 am: Spend a few hours eating.

10.45–11 am: Pick a spot, beat down the plants, and clear out a nice area to rest.

11 am–2 pm: Rest period. Young gorillas may play, others groom themselves, others sleep.

2–4 pm: Time for some more eating.

4–5 pm: Travel time. If the group has to move to a new site, this is the best time of day to do it.

5–7 pm: Once the leader has chosen a place to spend the night, it's nest-building time. All the nests need to be built by sunset.

Gorillas don't wander aimlessly from place to place. They live in an area called a **home range**. Each group stays in one large area of about 10 square kilometres. The home ranges of different groups can overlap. And gorillas are happy to let other animals share their home range. They don't defend their territory the way a dog might do. They just live in it. They travel a lot within the home range, mostly in search of food.

FACT FILE

Mountain gorillas make a new nest every night. It only takes a few minutes.

How to build a nest

1. Start as soon as the leader starts to make his nest. It's usually about an hour before sundown.

2. Break off any branches, herbs or other plants that look suitable.

3. Use them to make a circle, or half-circle, around the body. The base of the nest is not so important. It's the outside rim that really matters.

4. Then settle in! Sleep either on the side, with arms and legs tucked in, or on the stomach.

What do gorillas eat?

Mountain gorillas are very choosy eaters, so it takes them a while to find just the right kinds of food. They're very picky about the *part* of the plant they eat. Besides their favourite foods, they also eat stems and roots, and some berries and other fruit. They don't eat any meat, but occasionally dig open an ants' nest to eat the ants' eggs.

Gorillas rarely drink. Most of the liquid they get comes from the food itself. Each gorilla searches for its own food, except for the young who get help from adults.

FACT FILE

Here are the mountain gorilla's five favourite foods. You can find out what they are by unscrambling the captions. Do the pictures give you any clues? The answers are on page 32.

AMBOBO OTHOSS

WDIL LRYECE   TSELTHI

TENLETS

KARB

15

Where do gorillas live?

The area where an animal lives and eats is called its **habitat**. Gorillas can only survive in places where the specific plants they feed on are growing. There needs to be enough food for all of them.

The mountain gorilla's habitat is called the **tropical rain forest** (or, less scientifically, the jungle). A tropical rain forest is defined by its temperature and rainfall. Any place that is hot enough and wet enough can be called a tropical rain forest. In some places it rains – and is as hot as 27°C – all year round!

Tropical rain forests are full of epiphytes, plants that grow on other trees, branches and leaves. An orchid is a common epiphyte (say: epee-fite).

Tropical rain forests also contain lianas. These are climbing plants, like vines. They can be hundreds of metres long!

What is in a tropical rain forest?

There are many types of tropical rain forest. Mountain gorillas used to live mainly in mountain forests but now can be found even in the alpine forests, 1,000 metres higher up.

High in the mountains of the central African tropical rain forests, between 1300 and 3500 metres above sea level, there are both rainy and dry seasons. The weather is cool and often very misty. The average temperature is 9–12°C, and there is hail and frost. On average, about 200 cms of rain falls each year.

Alpine forest

At the top of the mountain, about 3500 metres and more above sea level, the forest becomes an alpine forest which looks more like a barren moonscape than a dense jungle. Mountain gorillas can be found even at this chilly height!

Hagenia and Hypericum forest

Between 2600 and 3500 metres above sea level, the forest is named after the two dominant plants, Hagenia and Hypericum. The hagenia forest is like the mountain forest but is more open, with smaller shrubs and herbs.

Bamboo forest

Higher up, at about 2500 metres, bamboo forests grow. The young bamboo shoots pop up during the heaviest rainy seasons, usually from October to December. The canopy is lower, about 4 to 6 metres high.

Mountain forest

At the bottom, the understorey is made up of plants and shrubs. There are herbs, ferns, mosses, and hundreds of other plants all densely packed together.

Next come the broadleaf evergreen trees, which are green all year round. Broadleaf trees have leaves, rather than needles like those on pine trees.

The tops of the trees grow together and form a canopy usually about 15 metres high. It's like a roof made of tree branches and leaves. If the canopy is really thick, not much sunlight or water reaches the understorey. Only hardy shrubs survive.

What is happening to the tropical rain forest?

People are cutting down the forest, and this is the major threat to the mountain gorilla's survival. Different countries have different reasons for doing this. Rwanda, for example, is the most heavily populated country in Africa. So Rwandans cleared the forest to make room for themselves, and to grow food and raise cattle. The bamboo and trees can also be burned as fuel or be used for building. Many of the people in these areas are poor and need to make money, so they have cleared the forest for timber or crops to export. Part of Rwanda's tropical forest was cleared to grow pyrethrum, a plant that is used to make insecticides that are sold in Europe.

But Rwanda is now conserving the forest. The country has realized that though clearing the forest may bring in money today, it will cost dearly tomorrow. The forest is a vital part of the environment. It helps prevent floods, mudslides and drought. It is also home to thousands of plants and animals.

FACT FILE
East Africa Facts at a Glance

RWANDA
Area: 26,338 square kilometres
Population: 7,603,000
Average density: 288 people per square kilometre
Capital: Kigali
Main industries: Agriculture, livestock
Exports: Coffee, tea, sugar, pyrethrum, tin, quinine

ZAIRE
Area: 2,345,409 square kilometres
Population: 35,330,000
Average density: 15 people per square kilometre
Capital: Kinshasa
Main industry: Palm oil production
Exports: Coffee, rubber, cocoa, timber, copper, crude oil

UGANDA
Area: 236,036 square kilometres
Population: 17,593,000
Average density: 75 people per square kilometre
Main industries: Agriculture, chemicals
Capital: Kampala
Main export: Coffee

The average density in the UK is 232 per sq. km. or 601 people per sq. mile.

The average density in the US is 26 per sq. km. or 68 people per sq. mile.

In a typical mountain forest, the canopy acts as an umbrella and stops the soil getting drenched.

Some of the water held in the canopy and roots evaporates and turns into rain again. In areas where the forest has been cleared, there's been a lot less rain. In the long term, less rain means droughts.

The roots soak up water and let it seep out slowly. They also hold the soil together to prevent mudslides and keep the rivers from flooding too much during the rainy season.

Can the gorillas survive?

As the tropical forest is cleared, the gorillas have fewer places to live and less food to eat. Many problems arise from these difficult conditions:

- If more groups are forced to live in a smaller area, they'll be forced to compete for food. This would affect their naturally peaceful way of life.

- Gorillas can't cross rivers or lakes because they can't swim. This stops them travelling long distances to find new homes.

- Every year gorillas die from diseases associated with humans, like malaria, pneumonia, and hookworm. Infants are usually hit hardest. Gorillas could be affected by disease even more with the strain of adapting to a new home.

- As the mountain gorillas are forced higher and higher into the mountains, the colder climate adds to the number of illnesses they already suffer from. More and more of them catch pneumonia.

- Mountain gorillas aren't good tree-climbers. If a gorilla is forced to climb a tree, it can fall out and hurt itself.

What else harms the gorillas?

The only animal gorillas have to beware of is MAN.

- Humans began hunting gorillas more than 100 years ago. Gorilla skins were sold to collectors, or displayed to show a hunter's bravery.

- Hunting for sport is less popular now. But poachers still trap gorillas and sell skulls and hands, made into ashtrays, as souvenirs.

- Poachers also hunt other animals in the forest. Gorillas can stumble into these traps and lose hands or feet. Some are forced into hiding, often into areas where they can't find food.

FACT FILE

Here are six different animals and six groups of products that are made from parts of their bodies. Match the product to the animal. The answers are on page 32.

Do you think these products are necessary? Can you think of substitutes for them?

What's being done to help mountain gorillas?

The future of the mountain gorilla is looking brighter, thanks to the work of private organizations and the governments of the African nations concerned. However, the mountains where most of them live are spread across three separate countries each of which has its own policy towards gorillas.

RWANDA

In 1979, animal scientists and concerned people from around the world joined together to form the Mountain Gorilla Project. This group works with Rwandans to study and protect mountain gorillas. They travel round showing films, and meeting people in schools and villages. They discuss gorillas, what can be done to help them, and how important it is to preserve their habitat.

The area where gorillas live is called the Parc National des Volcans, or Volcanoes National Park. It is a gorilla reserve. Poaching is forbidden, but though it is claimed that there has been no poaching since 1983 the laws are hard to enforce.

ZAIRE AND UGANDA

Both countries have formed groups similar to the Mountain Gorilla Project. The 300 mountain gorillas who live in Uganda's Bwindi Forest National Park seem fairly safe. The forest is so dense and thick that it's difficult for any people to live or work there, including poachers.

In the areas of the Parc National des Volcans that belong to Uganda and Zaire, there is less poaching now than there used to be. But some poachers still capture babies and sell them to zoos, and adult gorillas can sometimes get hurt or killed trying to defend their young.

Why would a zoo buy from poachers? Sometimes, someone will bring them a baby that's already been captured, so they have to take it in to keep it alive. Also, a few people believe that the best way to help the gorillas survive is to breed them in zoos, so that if gorillas in the wild die out, there will be enough gorillas in zoos to start a new population. But most gorilla scientists disagree with this idea.

FACT FILE

These are the goals of the various gorilla projects.

Goal: Continue to work against poaching.

Goal: Keep a close watch over the gorilla population.

Goal: Educate the local people about the gorillas and the need to protect them.

Goal: Encourage tourists to come and visit the gorillas, to raise money to help them.

What's it like on a gorilla watch?

Imagine sitting within touching distance of real live mountain gorillas, breathing in their scent and watching the babies at play.

Each year, more and more people go to Rwanda and Zaire to do just that. A guide takes small groups of people up into the mountains where several groups of gorillas will now let people come close to them.

These trips have become so popular that tourism is now one of Rwanda's three largest industries!

FACT FILE
NOTES

Clothes list:

Long trousers
Hiking boots
Long-sleeved shirt
Rain jacket
Lightweight gloves

They told us not to bring anything that could get tangled up in branches. And though it'll be hot we'll need to protect our arms and legs from the trees and bushes. A pullover will help as it feels chilly when you stop hiking.

DAY ONE

Flew to Kigali, the capital of Rwanda, then spent half a day driving through the cleared jungle to get to the park headquarters at Kinigi. There are six of us in my group and six in another group. There were no young children. I think the guides are concerned that children might be scared, or might scare the gorillas!

DAY TWO

Started our hike up the mountain. It took several hours, and was very hard work, because it was wet and we climbed to about 2500 metres (8000 feet).

At the park edge, we were trained in what to do when faced with an angry gorilla. If you feel afraid, or if the gorilla seems angry or aggressive, you should kneel and keep your head down. You should always move slowly. This makes the gorilla feel superior. Also, never get between two gorillas, especially a mother and her baby!

DAY THREE

Some other tips: no flash photography; don't touch the gorillas or let them touch you; don't point at a gorilla; and don't leave any litter!

We hiked to where the gorilla group had last been sighted. The guide told us to keep low and stay behind him. We tracked the group to find the nests and where they had spent the night. We finally found them about two hours' walk from there.

There were ten gorillas in the group. They didn't seem surprised or afraid of us. They looked at us, but didn't really move. The silverback looked huge, as if he would be bigger and much heavier than a tall man if he stood upright.

We watched them eat and sleep. The young ones played and wrestled with each other. One gorilla came up to smell me. He got so close that I could see the hairs on his chest. We looked at each other with curiosity and, I think, friendship. It wasn't till he walked away that I realized I had been holding my breath!

Why save mountain gorillas?

Here are some good reasons for making sure the mountain gorilla survives:

● Destroying the tropical rain forest is bad for everybody in the long run. Our environment is made up of many parts that all depend on each other. If some of those parts are taken away, the system doesn't work as well.

● As many kinds of birds and animals as possible must be allowed to survive. Saving the tropical forest for gorillas means saving it for many other kinds of birds and animals.

● Humans can learn a lot about themselves by studying gorillas and the great apes. They are our closest relatives in the animal kingdom.

● Some people believe that no animal, including man, should do things that harm other living things unless they have absolutely no alternative.

● Poachers should not be allowed to kill gorillas for fun, or to sell as souvenirs.

What can we do to help?

• Write to the governments of Rwanda, Zaire and Uganda, telling them what you've learned, and asking them to help the gorillas as much as they can.

• Write to the animal groups that work to protect gorillas, and give them your support.

• Try fund-raising with your friends. Ask if you can set up collection boxes in a local library or shops to raise money to help, or organize a sponsored gorilla walk.

• You and your parents could volunteer to be collectors for the World Wide Fund for Nature flag day.

• Anything you do to help is worthwhile. And remember, once you help support or protect an endangered animal, you become a real Wildlifer.

FACT FILE

Here are the addresses of some of the groups that help gorillas:

African Wildlife Foundation
1717 Massachusetts Avenue, N.W.
Washington, D.C. 20036
U.S.A.

World Wide Fund for Nature/United Kingdom
Panda House, Weyside Road
Godalming, Surrey GU7 1XR
ENGLAND

The Digit Fund
45 Inverness Drive East
Englewood, Colorado 80112-5430
U.S.A.

The Young People's Trust for Endangered Species
8 Leapale Road
Guildford, Surrey GU1 4JX
ENGLAND

Why don't you write to one of these groups? They could give you more information about mountain gorillas, and tell you how you could help them.

58

Catch flu, go back to ㊷

59

60

Homeland declared a National Park

48

49

57

Rangers catch poachers

50

56

55

54

44

Come to river, take detour

51

43 Land cleared for crops, go back to ㊳

52

53

42

41

22

21

20

Take a nap, miss a turn 23

24

25

Feed well on bamboo, move on to ㉒ 19

18

13

14

15

Meet tourists & behave well, move on to ㉕ 16

17

Index

Answers

Page 6-7:
The western lowland gorilla is C
The eastern lowland gorilla is A
The mountain gorilla is B

Page 9:
5 foot prints = 500
9 thumb prints = 90
4 knuckle prints = 4
Total: 594

Page 10-11:
Minimum number = 4
Maximum number = 8

Page 15:
Bamboo shoots; wild celery; thistle; nettles; bark.

Page 22-23:
Gorillas – hand and skull ashtrays
Crocodiles – handbags and shoes
Black Rhino and Elephants – ivory carvings and dagger handles
Sea Turtle – bracelets, combs
Spotted Cats – fur coats

Alternatives
Hand and skull ashtrays – totally unnecessary
Handbags and shoes – canvas, vinyl, rubber, nylon
Ivory dagger handles, carvings } plastic, wood
Bracelets, combs
Fur coats – fur fabric